There Has To Be More

Moving Beyond the Now

Darius L. Francis

Copyright © 2019 by **Darius L. Francis**

All rights reserved. No part of this publication may be reproduced, distributed, or transmitted in any form or by any means, without prior written permission.

Unless otherwise noted, all Scripture quotations are taken from The Holy Bible, New International Version®, NIV®. Copyright © 1973, 1978, 1984, 2011 by Biblica, Inc.™ Used by permission. All rights reserved worldwide.
Scripture quotations marked (BSB) are taken from The Holy Bible, Berean Study Bible, BSB. Copyright © 2016, 2018 by Bible Hub. Used by Permission. All Rights Reserved Worldwide.
Scripture quotations marked (KJV) are taken from the King James Bible. Accessed on Bible Gateway. www.BibleGateway.com.
Scripture quotations marked (NKJV) are taken from the New King James Version®. Copyright © 1982 by Thomas Nelson, Inc. Used by permission. All rights reserved.
Sermon To Book
www.sermontobook.com

There Has To Be More / Darius L. Francis

ISBN-13: 978-1-945793-71-4
ISBN-10: 1-945793-71-6

Praise for *There Has To Be More*

D. L. Francis masterfully depicts a life of more and shows us his uncanny ability to connect the idea that trusting God for more ultimately puts His super on our natural. In order to receive more, one must create an atmosphere that will disconnect itself from the very idea of settling for less. Accept your humanity, live humbly, and trust God!

Montel Richardson
Senior Pastor, First Baptist Church of Campbellsville, KY

Pastor Francis provides hope, encouragement, and a needed reminder that God will never leave you or forsake you during hard times. You will find comfort as Pastor Francis shines the light of the Word of God, revealing that Jesus Christ has a plan for your life and is truly the only hope that brings everlasting peace.

Robert Stephens
Senior Pastor, The Grace Center, Miami Gardens, FL

As people of faith, we must remember: no matter how helpless or hopeless our situations appear to us, God always requires us to seek Him and exercise more! Pastor Darius Francis is tenacious and determined in this book to point us in the direction of God's more. More faith, more prayer, more worship, and more of our Christian witness! This is a fresh read on a timeless truth.

Earl B. Payton, MDiv
Senior Pastor, SunCity Christian Fellowship Baptist Church, El Paso, TX

I'm reminded of the Parable of Talents and recognize that God has blessed D.L. Francis, indeed, with many talents. He did not bury them away, but he used all that God has given him and has moved self out of the way to give everything, and then some, back to God. As the words shared on these pages will pour into the lives of all those who read them, I trust that all the wisdom he has amassed will now be passed on and shared with every reader.

Everyone must take what they have been given and trust that it will work for their good, because everything that anyone needs is already inside of them. Realizing this, surely, they in turn will begin to look beyond the now and move into their awareness that "there has to be more"!

Davion Q. Crumel
Servant Leader, Antioch Missionary Baptist Church, Miami Gardens/Fort Lauderdale, FL

This book is going to bless the life of every reader like never before. You will find encouragement that will inspire you to trust God no matter where you are in your journey. You will close this book knowing and believing, just as my family and I did, that there shall be glory after this. To God be praise, blessings, and peace to my friend and beloved brother, Pastor D.L. Francis.

Martez J. Whipple Sr.
Senior Pastor, Mount Nebo Missionary Baptist Church, South Miami, FL

In times like these, when people are becoming stagnated and stuck in this thing called life, D.L. Francis has written a plan to help you to move beyond your now. He answers the question that many have asked themselves: "Is there more to this?" In this book, there are principles that will help you move from where you are to a place beyond your wildest dreams. It's a must-read for people from all walks of life.

Bishop Dexter L. Johnson
Senior Pastor, Higher Ground Empowerment Church, Atlanta, GA

As people, we have a threefold existence: a past, a present, and a future. Our past taught us principles. Our present ignites our potential. Our future gives us promise.

For me, my threefold life is broken down by three people: my grandmother, my mother, and my daughter.

My grandmother represents my past because she gave me the tools to be the man I am today. She taught me to seek and know the Lord with all my heart, mind, and soul. She has gone on to be with the Lord, but her legacy will live on through me.

My mother represents my present. She ignites the flame in me to burn brighter each day. She pushes and motivates me to chase after all that God has for me. Her support of my ministry is unparalleled. She was the first person I ever pastored. She has followed me across the country to support what she saw God doing in my life.

My daughter, nine years old, is the apple of my eye. She is my essence incarnated. She reminds me of how thirsty and hungry I was for life at her age. She has taught me to be gentler and warmer. She opened a part of my heart that I never knew I had, a place of pure and unconditional love.

This book is dedicated to Rosa Lee Moore, my grandmother; Carmelita McCray, my mother; and D'Shyla Francis, my daughter—the past, present, and future of my existence.

CONTENTS

Foreword by Dr. Emanuel Whipple Sr. 1
God Wants More of You— and More *for* You 3
Overcoming Our Attitudes 7
Do I Have What It Takes? 21
Clinging to Failure 33
Frustration and Burnout 45
Developing Our Negatives 59
Grace for the Race 67
The Lord Is on Your Side 81
Notes 85
About the Author 87
About Sermon To Book 89

FOREWORD

Foreword by Dr. Emanuel Whipple Sr.

Observation has taught me that people tend to end up in loneliness and despair not because of pain but because of disappointment with pleasure. Being let down after anticipating an ultimate, fulfilling experience leads to deep disappointment. That's the reality Pastor D.L. Francis examines in his sobering book.

I have known Pastor Francis for many years as one of my upcoming sons in the ministry. I appreciate his passion. His enthusiasm is contagious. His answers are practical. His love for God and people is refreshing, coming from a young man who has a mission and a message for reaching the unreachable. This book will help you move from pain and pleasure to a passion for experiencing *more*.

Dr. Emanuel Whipple Sr., Th.D.
Senior Pastor, Calvary Baptist Church of San Diego, CA

INTRODUCTION

God Wants More of You— and More *for* You

Picture this:

You're sitting at a card table, working on a one-thousand-piece jigsaw puzzle. You've been piecing this puzzle together for four nights now, tearing yourself away long past bedtime when your eyes start to cross. You're close, so close, with probably less than a dozen pieces left to fill in, when you notice the problem: You're missing a piece!

If you're a jigsaw puzzle fanatic, as I am, you slap the table with your palm, groan, and say, "No! *No!* There has to be more!" Then you spend the next hour on your knees, looking for the one that got away.

On a more significant level, imagine that you're sitting beside a hospital bed, praying the same prayer you've prayed for the last four nights before falling asleep in that uncomfortable recliner in the corner. Your loved one is close to a breakthrough. You can feel it, even if you can't see it—and then the latest test results come back. They're not good. Do you whisper to the Lord at 2 a.m., with a catch in your throat, "No! There has to be more than this"?

There *is* more. Perhaps you will not receive your answer immediately or in the form you want, but consider His Word, His promises to you.

> The LORD himself goes before you and will be with you; he will never leave you nor forsake you. Do not be afraid; do not be discouraged.
> **—Deuteronomy 31:8**

> "For I know the plans I have for you," declares the LORD, "plans to prosper you and not to harm you, plans to give you hope and a future. Then you will call on me and come and pray to me, and I will listen to you. You will seek me and find me when you seek me with all your heart."
> **—Jeremiah 29:11–13**

The "more" that God offers you is hinged to your relationship with Him. It is activated by answers to your prayers in ways you may have never considered. He offers you peace, deliverance, strength, and grace. You don't have to wander through life, merely hoping for the best and avoiding the worst.

If you want more in this life—if you *really* want it—it is here for the receiving. Many of us settle for less. It's easier, and everyone around us is settling, too. But if you want God's best, and you want it deeply, the Lord will honor your desire.

My spiritual father, Dr. Emanuel Whipple Sr., taught me something valuable in ministry. I joined his church when I was fifteen years old, after I had accepted my call to the preaching ministry. He took me in as one of his sons and pushed me to be better in ways I didn't know existed.

I was hungry for God at a young age. Growing up in a fixed-income home, I had a desire to experience more from life. I had the foundational relationship with God, but I did not know where to go from there. Dr. Whipple helped me understand that you can be your biggest hindrance in life. Oftentimes we blame God, but is it really God? Who's really holding us back?

God never changes. He is the same today as He was at the moment when He spoke the universe into being (Hebrews 13:8). In this book, we will explore the ways God provided for several men across history in the Bible and how He changed them in the process—the same way He wants to provide for and change you today.

My hope is that you will find encouragement in these pages to:

- Follow the Lord's plan, and no one else's, for victory in the battles you face;
- Remember that you have all you need, all it takes, to follow Jesus and obey Him;
- Passionately pursue God's best;
- Stay the course even when the waiting gets hard; and
- Offer praise for God's grace even in trials.

At the end of each chapter, application-focused workbook sections will help you dig into the truths in the list above. As you read this book, may God grant you His grace as you seek the "more" He has for you, your family, your church, and your community.

CHAPTER ONE

Overcoming Our Attitudes

Read Judges 6 and 7.

Let's begin our Bible journey with Gideon, in the book of Judges. During this time in Israel's history, they had turned away from God time after time and worshiped Baal, the god of the Amorites. God sent them leaders, known as judges, to rescue them and bring them back to Him over and over, even though they had disobeyed. The cycle seemed endless: disobedience, rescue, a time of peace, then disobedience again.

In Gideon's time, it was the Midianites who were oppressing Israel, stealing their food and livestock and leaving them with nothing to eat. When God called Gideon to save Israel from the Midianites, He was essentially saying, "The Israelites are still Mine. They're oppressed, they're dispossessed, and they're overwhelmed, but they are still Mine."

Gideon's story begins with him hiding in a winepress to thresh his wheat so the Midianites couldn't steal it

(Judges 6:11). He was in a grumpy mood and felt powerless to change his situation. As far as he was concerned, his ancestors' stories of miracles were overblown. He hadn't seen a miracle in his lifetime, nor had any of his friends. He was sick of working so hard and still not having enough to eat.

> When the angel of the LORD appeared to Gideon, he said, "The LORD is with you, mighty warrior."
>
> "Pardon me, my lord," Gideon replied, "but if the LORD is with us, why has all this happened to us? Where are all his wonders that our ancestors told us about when they said, 'Did not the LORD bring us up out of Egypt?' But now the LORD has abandoned us and given us into the hand of Midian."
>
> The LORD turned to him and said, "Go in the strength you have and save Israel out of Midian's hand. Am I not sending you?"
>
> "Pardon me, my lord," Gideon replied, "but how can I save Israel? My clan is the weakest in Manasseh, and I am the least in my family."
>
> —Judges 6:12–15

One thing I love about Scripture is that it portrays people the way they really are, warts and all. Because of this, we can learn from their mistakes as well as their victories. Gideon's knee-jerk response to God's call was to look at the circumstances, not God. He challenged God for abandoning Israel. When that didn't work, he switched to arguing about his own weakness and lack of position. He even doubted that the call was from God.

Have you ever found yourself in a similar situation, complaining about the circumstances rather than believing God for the answer? The problem was that Gideon doubted his abilities. You may doubt yours, too.

The fact is that God will never ask you to do anything for which He does not equip you. You can dwell on your past or your family position, but in truth, you are "fearfully and wonderfully made" (Psalm 139:14) in the image of a perfect God (Genesis 1:27). Like Gideon, you need to get past your doubts and learn to trust in God and your relationship with Him.

Gideon asked for signs. Notice that God did not get angry at Gideon. Instead, He gave Gideon what he asked for in order to reassure him:

> Gideon said to God, "If you will save Israel by my hand as you have promised—look, I will place a wool fleece on the threshing floor. If there is dew only on the fleece and all the ground is dry, then I will know that you will save Israel by my hand, as you said." And that is what happened. Gideon rose early the next day; he squeezed the fleece and wrung out the dew—a bowlful of water.
>
> Then Gideon said to God, "Do not be angry with me. Let me make just one more request. Allow me one more test with the fleece, but this time make the fleece dry and let the ground be covered with dew." That night God did so. Only the fleece was dry; all the ground was covered with dew.
> **—Judges 6:36–40**

Still today, we talk about "putting out a fleece" to verify something that we believe God is telling us.

Finally convinced, Gideon gathered an army of 32,000 men to fight the Midianites. This would have been impressive, except for the fact that the Midianite army had more than 120,000 swordsmen. If those odds weren't good by human reasoning, the Lord made them worse. He told Gideon to send home any man who was afraid to fight. The army was reduced to 10,000 (Judges 7:2–3).

Why did God want fewer men to fight? He didn't want Gideon's army to think that they had won the battle in their own strength (Judges 7:2). Israel needed a miracle so that the people would return to God. He needed them to know that the victory was all because of Him.

To Gideon's dismay, the Lord required yet another test to sort out those not fit for battle.

> But the LORD said to Gideon, "There are still too many men. Take them down to the water, and I will thin them out for you there. If I say, 'This one shall go with you,' he shall go; but if I say, 'This one shall not go with you,' he shall not go."
>
> So Gideon took the men down to the water. There the LORD told him, "Separate those who lap the water with their tongues as a dog laps from those who kneel down to drink." Three hundred of them drank from cupped hands, lapping like dogs. All the rest got down on their knees to drink.
>
> The LORD said to Gideon, "With the three hundred men that lapped I will save you and give the Midianites into your hands. Let all the others go home."
>
> —*Judges 7:4–7*

Why on earth did the Lord reduce the army to a measly three hundred soldiers? The Lord knew that then every man in Gideon's army would be a true soldier. God—and Gideon—needed people who would fight when it was time to fight.

In your life, you must also be careful whom you take into battle with you. Not everyone who stands by your side is on your side. Some have ulterior motives. Some have too much jealousy in their hearts. Some have too many wounds of their own, and they can't pick up a sword on your behalf. Some want all of the attention—even to the point of walking with you to the front lines, then walking away with your crown when you get shot down. Fewer is better when those few have your back.

Maybe the Lord is allowing your circumstances to grow so hopeless that only He can solve the problems. That way you'll know when the victory comes that it is from His hand. Your friends may desert you because they don't want to get involved. They may think that they're leaving behind a mangled, miserable mess, but then they will see God bring you through to the other side.

Let me offer you a warning that may sound counterintuitive: Sometimes your friends are really your enemies and your enemies are really your friends. With whom do you fall into sin? Your friends. Who keeps you on your toes and praying at the feet of Jesus? Your enemies. Sometimes your enemy is the reason you are staying so focused on God and your friend is the reason you wander.

Like Gideon, you need people who are prepared to go into battle with you—for the right reasons. You need those who will cry with you, then fight with you, and sometimes even fight for you.

Walking into Victory

Now that Gideon had his army set, the Lord gave him the battle plan. He told Gideon to go down to the Midianite camp at night and listen to what they were saying

(Judges 7:9–11).

> *Gideon arrived just as a man was telling a friend his dream. "I had a dream," he was saying. "A round loaf of barley bread came tumbling into the Midianite camp. It struck the tent with such force that the tent overturned and collapsed."*
>
> *His friend responded, "This can be nothing other than the sword of Gideon son of Joash, the Israelite. God has given the Midianites and the whole camp into his hands."*
> —*Judges 7:13–14*

See how merciful the Lord is? He had already told Gideon that He would give him victory over the Midianites, but He reassured him yet again. Gideon was so convinced that "he bowed down and worshiped" (Judges 7:15).

The truth of the matter is that it's hard to receive the victory when you haven't first believed the victory. Oftentimes when we struggle with overcoming our situations and circumstances, it's not because God doesn't want us to be victorious. We struggle to overcome because we don't see in ourselves what God sees in us.

I recall when I first started wrestling in middle school. One particular match I remember vividly. It was my seventh match. My record was currently 0–6. I had lost literally every match thus far, so losing wasn't new to me. I had become accustomed to losing. After all, most of my opponents had been wrestling since the sixth grade, and this was my first year—and I was on varsity.

I tried to give this particular match all I had. It lasted longer than any other match I had ever been in. We were both novices, and at the end of the match, we were tied for points. They sent the match into overtime, which meant that the next point or pin would take the victory. In wrestling, you get points for each position you place your opponent into and every position you get yourself out of.

My coach told me before overtime started, "You need to stay dominant. All you need to do is grab him and hold on!" I got back on the mat and did just that. As soon as I grabbed him and established dominance, I received three points and won the match. I got up from the mat, exhausted. Those five minutes felt like five hours, but I won.

So often when we find ourselves wrestling with situations and circumstances in life, we never get the results we want because we don't hold on long enough. God's Word will never return to Him "void" (Isaiah 55:11 KJV). The promises of the Lord are "Yes" and "Amen" (2 Corinthians 1:20). What are you holding on to? Galatians 6:9 tells us that "in due season we shall reap, if we faint not" (KJV).

You must trust the Lord's leading. You must trust the Lord to give you the victory. But you also need His touch, His reassurance. The Lord understood Gideon's concerns and fears of getting it right. He also understands yours.

Don't be afraid to ask the Lord for His reassurance as many times as you need it. Then be ready to obey whatever He tells you to do, even if it's not the way you would do it yourself. The final battle plan God gave to Gideon was certainly unique:

> The LORD said to Gideon, "With the three hundred men that lapped I will save you and give the Midianites into your hands. Let all the others go home." So Gideon sent the rest

> *of the Israelites home but kept the three hundred, who took over the provisions and trumpets of the others.*
> —*Judges 7:7–8a*

Read that last part again: "the three hundred ... took over the ... trumpets of the others" (Judges 7:8). Why on earth would Gideon give each soldier a second trumpet? Because they were going to double their praise! The praise they gave the Lord before the battle wouldn't match the level of praise they would give Him after the victory. These soldiers—abandoned by those too afraid to fight, set apart from those mentally unprepared for the fight—would take the trumpets of their former comrades and use them to praise the Lord.

When people leave our lives, we shouldn't use that as an opportunity to bash them or belittle them. God makes no mistakes. There are times when people who come into your life will leave an impact only with their departure. When they leave, you will realize that they left behind a trumpet. They gave you a reason and a means to praise God. Hindsight will show you that they pushed you into a place where your hunger and thirst for God and the things of God increased to a new level, and you will praise the Lord for all of His orchestration.

When the Lord gives you and me the victory, we will need two trumpets to praise Him. You won't praise God the same way you did before. When the Lord brings you through a major breakthrough, it calls for major worship.

The breakthrough will happen when you simply walk into the victory the Lord has won for you. Consider what the Israelites experienced at the end of Judges 7.

> "Watch me," he told them. "Follow my lead. When I get to the edge of the camp, do exactly as I do. When I and all who are with me blow our trumpets, then from all around the camp blow yours and shout, 'For the LORD and for Gideon.'"
> —Judges 7:17–18

As the men followed Gideon into the sleeping camp, they all blew their trumpets and held up their lights at Gideon's signal. The Midianites were terrified and panicked. They even drew their swords and started killing each other! Then the Midianite army fled, with Gideon and those he gathered from the rest of Ephraim in hot pursuit.

What did Gideon and his soldiers do? Did they fight furiously, courageously, desperately, unreservedly? No. They simply followed Gideon's instructions. The Lord did the work, and they walked into the victory. Israel had witnessed a miracle from God and once again gave up worshiping Baal and other false gods.

Gideon is often remembered for his doubt and reluctance. This is somewhat of a misrepresentation because when Gideon did take up God's call to battle, he became an effective leader and soldier. After he expelled the Midianites from the land, Gideon became one of Israel's judge-leaders, ruling for forty years.

The Lord goes ahead of us in ways we often never see. He wants to keep us close to Him. We belong to Him, and the victory will be ours because of Him.

In the next chapter, we will move ahead from the time of the judges to the reign of Israel's first king, Saul. There, we will see another man fight another battle and demonstrate great faith in facing an obstacle of truly gigantic proportions.

WORKBOOK

Chapter One Questions

Question: Why did Gideon doubt God's willingness to rescue His people? When has God rescued you from bondage of your own making? Why did Gideon doubt his ability to fulfill God's call? What has God called you to do that is beyond your own abilities?

_____

_____

_____

_____

_____

_____

_____

_____

Question: Why did God shrink Gideon's already outnumbered army? What are some types of people you should not rely on in spiritual warfare? Are your friends encouraging you to obey God or to do your own thing?

_____

_____

_____

_____

_____

_____

_____

_____

_____

Question: What were some ways God reassured Gideon that this seemingly crazy plan was indeed from Him? How have you experienced God's comforting confirmation?

_____

_____

_____

_____
_____
_____
_____
_____
_____
_____
_____
_____

Action: Get your second trumpet ready! Begin now to praise God for the victory you already have over sin and death. Thank Him in advance for the victory you trust Him to give you in the specific battles you face today.

Chapter One Notes

CHAPTER TWO

Do I Have What It Takes?

Read 1 Samuel 17:1–51.

A champion named Goliath stepped out of the Philistine ranks and growled, "This day I defy the armies of Israel! Give me a man and let us fight each other" (1 Samuel 17:10). According to 1 Samuel 17:4, Goliath's "height was six cubits and a span." Taking a cubit to be about eighteen inches and a span to equal six inches, he was approximately nine feet, six inches tall. Some texts put him at four cubits plus a span. Either way, he was huge! And he was armored to the hilt.

> *He had a bronze helmet on his head and wore a coat of scale armor of bronze weighing five thousand shekels; on his legs he wore bronze greaves, and a bronze javelin was slung on his back. His spear shaft was like a weaver's rod, and its iron point weighed six hundred shekels.*
> —*1 Samuel 17:5–7a*

To a man, the Israelites were terrified (1 Samuel 17:11). No one had the nerve to face the giant one on one. Worse yet, the winner would take all (1 Samuel 17:9).

The Israelites and the Philistines had been sworn enemies for years. They faced each other, ready for battle. The Israelites had already won three out of five battles with the Philistines, and they were the chosen people of God. The Philistines had only won one battle thus far, but this time they were certain that they couldn't lose. There's no question that Goliath was the Philistines' golden bullet.

David's Humility and Obedience

It is easy to forget David's humble beginnings as a shepherd, considered the least of his father Jesse's sons (1 Samuel 16:10–13). Shepherds of his time had very low status. They were away from the rest of the family for extended periods of time, and they often slept in tents. To top it off, they probably stank from lack of personal hygiene, wearing the same clothes for days, and living in close proximity to their charges.

Now introduce this shepherd to the battlefield crisis.

Three of David's brothers were serving in King Saul's army at the time (1 Samuel 17:13–15) and had witnessed Goliath's challenge. David had once again been left behind to watch the stinking sheep. David was the youngest, and if you're the youngest, you know that this happens all too regularly. You tend to get left behind with the chores (and the clothes, the toys, the beat-up car) that nobody else wants.

It got worse. Adding insult to injury, David's father,

Jesse, told him to take his brothers some food (1 Samuel 17:17–19). What a humiliating, insignificant assignment. "Son, you don't get to fight with the big boys, but here, take them some sandwiches, okay?"

David didn't chafe at or complain about his assignment. He simply obeyed. Think about what happens when the Lord gives you some puny task. Do you feel insulted? David didn't resent a simple assignment, but in our culture, we often do. We despise small beginnings (Zechariah 4:10). We don't want to start at the bottom and work our way up. This is not the way God thinks. God starts with the small.

How you handle the small assignments reveals a lot about your character: "Whoever can be trusted with very little can also be trusted with much, and whoever is dishonest with very little will also be dishonest with much" (Luke 16:10). Those who are faithful with little will be given more. Jesse gave David a simple task. Because David was obedient, God took his simple task and turned it into a supernatural feat.

David's Faith

All of the Israelites were quaking in their sandals with fear of this giant, who was railing against them and their God. David arrived on the scene, bringing the missing ingredient: faith. David brought faith into a sea of fear. He said, "Forget about Goliath. Let me tell you about my God."

The Israelites were justified in their fear when they left God out of the equation. There is so much fear and insecurity in our world today when we leave God out of the picture. Many people are starving to hear words that bolster their courage and resolve.

If you know of people who are full of fear, God needs you to bring your faith to them. Tell them, "I once was young and now am old, yet never have I seen the righteous abandoned..." (Psalm 37:25 BSB). Say to them, "The LORD is the everlasting God, the Creator of the ends of the earth. He will never grow faint or weary; His understanding is beyond searching out. He gives power to the faint and increases the strength of the weak" (Isaiah 40:28–29 BSB).

Whether you're experiencing fear within yourself or you see it in someone else, faith is the answer. Faith that God is with you and that He is able and willing to handle any situation you face will take you from a place of fear to a place of courage and victory.

David's Discouraging Dilemma

David brought the answer to their dilemma. Nevertheless, everyone around David discounted him. After all, this teenage boy running around the camp couldn't know anything about a real battle. All he knew was sheep. He was still wet behind the ears.

David's oldest brother overheard him and said, "Why have you come down here? And with whom did you leave those few sheep in the wilderness? I know how conceited you are and how wicked your heart is; you came down only to watch the battle" (1 Samuel 17:28).

As if that weren't enough, King Saul even pulled him

aside and said, "You are not able to go out against this Philistine and fight him; you are only a young man, and he has been a warrior from his youth" (1 Samuel 17:33).

But David wasn't buying it. He knew his God's power and faithfulness. Just because he was young didn't mean that he was naïve or inexperienced. He had been through tough things. He had known pain; he had cried. He had even killed a lion and a bear to save his sheep (1 Samuel 17:34–37). He had God's authority. If God empowered him to kill the lion and the bear, what threat was a Philistine? David knew God, and God knew David.

At this point, Samuel had already secretly anointed David to be Israel's next king (1 Samuel 16:1–13). Only David's family knew this, but David had zero doubt that God would keep His promise to him. No Philistine could kill David. David was going to be king, and he knew that he had much to learn before he was ready to rule a nation.

David was anointed at age 15, but not appointed until age 30. If you haven't reached your destiny, it doesn't mean that you're not anointed. Don't be discouraged by the delay. All it means is that the anointing is developing your character. You can relax and give God time to get you ready.

There was one final discounting of David. Saul finally agreed to let David fight Goliath, but he first insisted that David wear all of the typical armor of the time (1 Samuel 17:37–39). But when David tried it on, he couldn't even move in all of that heavy gear, so he took it off.

He didn't need it. He was already wearing the armor of God: the "belt of truth," the "breastplate of righteousness," the "shield of faith," and the "helmet of salvation"

(Ephesians 6:13–17). He cloaked himself in the power of prayer and supplication in the Spirit (Ephesians 6:18). All David needed was his sling and five smooth stones.

David's Daring

Why did David bring five stones? Did he think that it might take five to bring the Philistine down? No. David knew that God would give him the victory over Goliath, just as God had given him the victory over the lion and the bear. You don't get a second shot if you miss a charging bear or a crouching lion! I believe David took five stones instead of one because he knew that Goliath had a brother and three sons. He was prepared for more battles, if need be.

Do you follow me? Don't giants in our lives seem to come in families?

- The doctor says that they've done all they can do for you. But you are healed by the stripes of Jesus (Isaiah 53:5 BSB), so pick up that second stone.

- It seems that everything and everybody has the worst timing, and you are struggling with patience. "But they that wait upon the LORD shall renew their strength" (Isaiah 40:31 KJV), so pick up that third stone.

- You've been drinking tears instead of water, crying all night into the midnight hour. "But joy comes in the morning" (Psalm 30:5 BSB), so pick up that fourth stone.

- It may seem as though there is trouble on the left and hell on the right. "Many are the afflictions of the righteous, but the LORD delivers him from them all" (Psalm 34:19 BSB), so pick up that fifth stone.

David dared to approach Goliath with five stones, ready to knock down every giant he might encounter in the name and the power of the God of Israel. David knew that he was more than a conqueror (Romans 8:37), that no weapon forged against him would prevail (Isaiah 54:17), that he would not die but live, and that he would proclaim what the LORD had done (Psalm 118:17).

David's faith was not in vain:

As the Philistine moved closer to attack him, David ran quickly toward the battle line to meet him. Reaching into his bag and taking out a stone, he slung it and struck the Philistine on the forehead. The stone sank into his forehead, and he fell facedown on the ground.

So David triumphed over the Philistine with a sling and a stone; without a sword in his hand he struck down the Philistine and killed him.

David ran and stood over him. He took hold of the Philistine's sword and drew it from the sheath. After he killed him, he cut off his head with the sword.

When the Philistines saw that their hero was dead, they turned and ran.

—1 Samuel 17:48–51

You don't need to be a future king to get God's notice and support. Approach your giants the same way. Follow David's example of humility, faith, courage, and confidence in God.

- Be obedient in every task, small or great.
- Fix your eyes on God, not on your giant. Trust in the Lord's anointing and His timing.
- Take up all the stones you need to finish the job. Defeat your giant in the power and name of our God.

After David killed Goliath, Saul called him into his service. Every campaign David was involved in succeeded, and he eventually became the commander of all of Saul's armies. Still, he never lost his humble perspective and love for his Maker. As a psalmist, he wrote:

> *I would rather be a doorkeeper in the house of my God than dwell in the tents of the wicked.*
> **—Psalm 84:10b**

So far, God proves to be consistent in the Old Testament! Moving on to the New Testament in the next chapter, we will look at how Jesus Himself responded to someone who was afraid to pursue the healing he desperately needed. It's amazing how tenaciously we can cling to the things we know, rather than accept God's offer of an infinitely better life.

WORKBOOK

Chapter Two Questions

Question: How did David's faithfulness in the menial job of shepherding prepare him for God's call to be a warrior? What are some small things God has called you to be faithful in right now?

_____
_____
_____
_____
_____
_____
_____
_____
_____
_____

Question: Why was David brave enough to face a giant no one else in the army dared to face? Where was his focus? Do you focus on your problems or on God's power? How can you keep the right focus?

_____
_____
_____
_____
_____
_____
_____
_____
_____

Question: What were the purpose and significance of David picking up five stones? Have you ever started on a task God called you to do but then not seen it through? What verses can encourage you to persevere?

_____
_____
_____
_____

_____

_____

_____

_____

_____

_____

_____

Action: Gather five smooth stones and put them on your desk, a shelf, or some other place where you will see them often. Let them be a tangible reminder that God's power is at work in and through you to face any and every giant in your life.

Chapter Two Notes

CHAPTER THREE

Clinging to Failure

Read John 5:1–15.

Bethesda was a pool in Jerusalem. It was near a city gate in the wall. Nobody went to Bethesda to take a bath, to get a drink, to lounge, to wash clothes, or to socialize. They went for one reason only: to be healed. People believed that every so often, an angel of the Lord would descend and stir the waters of the pool, and the first person in the water after it had been stirred would be healed of whatever sickness ailed him.

Can you imagine a city pool surrounded with nothing but sick people? This wasn't a hospital waiting room, where everybody was going to get a turn. This was a waiting game followed by a race to the water, and there was only one winner per stirring. Did these folks talk to one another to pass the time or help each other out? I doubt it. Every person was focused on his or her own healing.

One day, Jesus passed the pool on His way to attend a Jewish festival in Jerusalem. He learned about a man who had been crippled for thirty-eight years. When He saw the man lying by the pool, He asked him, "Do you want to get well?" (John 5:6).

It was a simple question. You'd think the man would have been ecstatic at the thought. Instead, he whined, "I have no one to help me into the pool when the water is stirred. While I am trying to get in, someone else goes down ahead of me" (John 5:7).

The invalid wanted to be sure that Jesus understood how difficult his life was. But Jesus had not asked him, "Why aren't you whole?" Jesus didn't ask whose fault it was, how he felt about being lame, or even how long he'd been lame. He simply asked the man if he wanted to be healed. Sickness had become normal; lying on the ground at the pool had become his daily ritual. Did he want to face such major changes in his life?

The pool of Bethesda parallels the church in some ways. The church is meant to be a place of healing, a place where the sick are welcomed. Jesus said that He came to call not the healthy, but the sick; not the righteous, but sinners (Luke 5:31–32).

The truth is that we're all sick. We all have wounded places that need healing and places of sin that need cleansing. It doesn't matter how long we've been following Jesus; every one of us needs His healing and cleansing touch.

Jesus can handle sickness. All it takes is His touch. The problem I see is that if you're sick and everybody around you is sick, as at the pool of Bethesda, then after a while, being sick becomes normal. You may resist any change for the better.

For example, if you like to swear and everybody you hang out with has an equally filthy mouth, eventually your foul mouth won't even register with you anymore. If you're chasing every unholy desire that raises its head and you're hanging out with other people who do the same thing, you will lose sight of what's holy.

Jesus wants you to come as you are, but He doesn't want to leave you sick. He wants to heal you. The question is: Do you want to be healed?

Check Your Perspective

If you have been coming to church year after year after year with the same sickness, you may have lost hope. Maybe you have watched others be healed and spent so much energy in envy that you've lost the will to pursue your own healing. Maybe you're so caught up in nursing your wounds and casting blame that you can't even look in the mirror anymore. Maybe you're just going through the motions.

How badly do you want healing, deliverance, or whatever else you need to be set free? Perhaps you've become too comfortable with the same familiar places, people, and habits that fill your life. The invalid in this passage was surrounded by sick people just like himself. How on earth could he ever get a different perspective? This man was so worried about his surroundings that he couldn't get past them.

Your surroundings have a lot to do with how long you stay in your situation. I have a challenge for you. If you are stuck in a place where you tolerate your sickness, get out. Whoever pulls you into thinking that your condition is normal—whether friends, family members, co-workers, or anyone else—you need to pull away from them. Focus your eyes on Jesus and His offer of healing, cleansing, and purpose. Pray for Him to work miracles on your behalf!

Change Your Position

What did Jesus say next to the invalid at the pool? "Get up! Pick up your mat and walk" (John 5:8). It didn't matter whether the water had been stirred or not. It didn't matter who got to the water first. It didn't matter how long he'd been lame or how long he'd been at the pool of Bethesda. What mattered was whether he was ready to change. Was he ready to stand up when he'd been down for so long? Was he ready to take Jesus at His word? Was he tired of his mundane life? Clearly, the decision was his. He had to obey and stand up or remain in his misery.

If you are tired of fighting through depression and anxiety resulting from the hand that life has dealt you, rise up and walk. Don't be passive. Rise up out of the dust and ashes of your pain and pressures. Rise up out of the clutches of your adversaries. Rise up out of poverty and persecution. Decide that you've had enough. You truly have to want the change.

I know for myself what a difference it can make to *really* want something. In 2011, I was stationed at Fort Campbell, Kentucky, as part of the 101st Airborne Division. As a 21-year-old specialist, I had been in the Army three years already, and it was time for me to go to the promotion board for advancement to sergeant.

I completed the board and was recommended for promotion, along with only one other soldier. However, because I was in an air assault division, I was told that I would have to complete air assault school to get promoted. Unfortunately, I had already been to air assault school twice—and was unsuccessful both times. But this time, with my promotion in the balance, I had additional motivation to succeed.

The school had three phases: air assault operations, setting up a pick-up zone and landing zone, and sling load operations. After these three phases were completed, on the morning of graduation, we had to complete a twelve-mile road march. The route was challenging, being significantly elevated and depressed at certain points. We had three hours to complete it.

I finished the first six miles in one hour and sixteen minutes. But when I reached the ninth mile, I twisted my ankle. As I lay there on the ground in agony and pain, I watched as many of the people behind me passed by me. Everyone faced the same strict time constraints, so no one attempted to assist me.

Finally, I heard one of the instructors call out for the field medical team. He told them that I was down and could not continue. Meanwhile, I thought to myself, "I can't fail now. I've come all this way, and this is the third time!"

He looked at me on the ground and saw the tears in my eyes. He kicked my weapon closer to me and asked, "How bad do you want it?"

I told him that I didn't want it. I *needed* it.

"Well, get up and finish!" he replied.

At that, I mustered the strength to climb to my feet. Though I couldn't walk properly, I limped the last three miles and managed to finish the march in two hours and forty-six minutes.

When I stopped looking at my circumstances and instead looked at the Lord, I found the strength I needed to carry on. I changed both my perspective and my position. Now I relive this lesson in faith whenever I need God's touch.

Have you been there? Have you been down, on your third try, wounded, watching everyone around you get to the goal, wondering if there was any way up or out?

God receives glory when others see the changes in us. When the man at Bethesda got up and walked, you can be sure that others noticed! The Pharisees asked him who had told him to pick up his mat and walk (John 5:12).

Amazingly, the man "had no idea who it was" (John 5:13). The Son of God had stood by his side and given him new life, but he hadn't even bothered to ask His name. Later, Jesus met him at the temple and said, "See, you are well again. Stop sinning or something worse may happen to you" (John 5:14).

When the man reported back to the Pharisees that Jesus had healed him, they were delighted—not that the man was healed, but that Jesus had dared to heal on the Sabbath. They had been looking for a way to accuse Jesus of wrongdoing. Now they had their ticket. Scripture is silent about the fate of the invalid, but the Pharisees' plot continued to grow until the Lord's crucifixion, thanks in part to this man's involvement.

Jesus gave His life to set you free. He is willing and

able to relieve your suffering. When you move on, be certain to give Him the glory. Give Him thanks and praise and your complete devotion. Remember not to let your guard down to sin, or you could fall into yet another trap of the enemy.

How badly do you want it?

- Do what Jesus commands. In His power, in His name, and at His direction, change your position.
- Get up. Don't focus on anyone else—what they have, where they are, or how they've treated you. Focus on getting yourself up, in the power of Jesus.
- Get out. Get away from those who hold you back and hold you down. There are plenty of sick people around the pool who will shove you aside in their own quest for healing.
- Follow Jesus. Walk only in His direction.
- Take up your mat. Make no provision for an easy retreat to where you had been stuck. While it was comfortable because it was familiar, it was also toxic.
- Give God glory, honor, and praise for the victory. Tell others so that they can praise Him, too.

Then say good-bye to Bethesda.

In the next chapter, we will look at the life of one of Jesus' disciples after Jesus' death on the cross. Surely, the disciples couldn't have had problems believing or obeying

God, could they? After all, they lived with the Son of God and were taught directly by Him, right?

WORKBOOK

Chapter Three Questions

Question: What problems have become so familiar to you that you no longer notice them? Are there people in your life who normalize your sin, sickness, or difficulties?

_____
_____
_____
_____
_____
_____
_____
_____
_____
_____
_____

Question: What thoughts do you imagine went through the lame man's mind when Jesus told him to "get up"? What seemingly impossible step of faith do you need to take to receive the blessings and obey the calling God has for you?

_____
_____
_____
_____
_____
_____
_____
_____
_____
_____

Question: What are some examples of a crippling or toxic comfort zone? How can a person who has spent a lifetime in such an environment walk away and find healing?

_____
_____
_____
_____

Action: Do you think that the lame man truly appreciated his healing? What attitudes might have held him back in an invalid mindset even after he was healed? What has Jesus done in your life that you can thank Him for today? Take time to write a testimony of gratitude for His work in your life.

Chapter Three Notes

CHAPTER FOUR

Frustration and Burnout

Read John 21:1–25.

Peter went fishing. That might not seem unusual. After all, Peter was a fisherman. But Peter and the other disciples had just seen the risen Lord, spoken with Him, heard His voice, and touched His body. If they had doubted or wondered or even just been confused about who Jesus was and what His ultimate mission was, surely that time had passed.

Jesus had told Peter and the other disciples to go to Galilee, where He would meet them. But when Peter got to Galilee, he went fishing (John 21:1–3). That is, he quit. The Greek word Peter used here is *hupago*, which literally means "I retire."[1] Clearly, Peter was ready to stop preaching and go back to his former life.

> *"I'm going out to fish," Simon Peter told them, and they said, "We'll go with you." So they went out and got into the boat, but that night they caught nothing.*
> —*John 21:3*

Perhaps Peter was tired of waiting for Jesus to show up in Galilee. Maybe he just didn't know what else to do. After all, he had denied the Lord three times (John 18:15–18, 25–27). Perhaps he felt that he no longer qualified to be a "fisher of men" (Matthew 4:18–20 NKJV).

During Jesus' earthly ministry, Peter was enthusiastic, adventurous, and committed. When Peter saw Jesus walking on water, he didn't just stare in awe—he had to try it out for himself (Matthew 14:25–31)! He was a strong man, a natural leader. He was impulsive and sometimes spoke or acted before he thought, but I picture Peter as warm, expansive, and fun to be around.

Peter reminds me so much of myself when I read about him in Scripture. When the Lord called me to ministry, I thought it was so that people would laugh in church. I always brought a lively, energetic spirit into the room. Even to this day, it still amazes me that God called a silly kid like me into the ministry of preaching His gospel. Isn't it awesome that the Lord can use your natural gifts and talents for a spiritual purpose and calling?

Jesus obviously thought that Peter was special. Peter was one of the first disciples Jesus called (Matthew 4:18–22). He drew Peter into His inner circle, along with James and John. These three were with Jesus in His most intimate moments: when He raised Jairus's daughter from the dead (Mark 5:35–43), at His transfiguration on the mountain (Luke 9:28–36), and during His agony in the Garden of Gethsemane before His crucifixion (Matthew 26:36–56).

Nearing the end of His ministry, Jesus asked His

disciples who they thought He was. Peter said, "You are the Messiah, the Son of the living God" (Matthew 16:16).

> *Jesus replied, "Blessed are you, Simon son of Jonah, for this was not revealed to you by flesh and blood, but by my Father in heaven. And I tell you that you are Peter, and on this rock I will build my church, and the gates of Hades will not overcome it. I will give you the keys of the kingdom of heaven; whatever you bind on earth will be bound in heaven, and whatever you loose on earth will be loosed in heaven."*
>
> **—Matthew 16:17–19**

Jesus had plans for Peter. He knew Peter's heart. When the Roman soldiers came to arrest Jesus in Gethsemane, Peter, trying to defend Him, cut off the ear of a servant of the high priest (John 18:10). Peter even told Jesus that he was willing to die with Him (Luke 22:31–33). Then he denied Jesus—not once, but three times. At that moment, a look from Jesus broke his heart, and he "wept bitterly" (Luke 22:61–62).

Peter was not new to the life of following Jesus. He wasn't new to the miracles, to the resistance of the authorities, to the suffering and persecution, to the awe and wonder. But now Peter didn't know the next step. He had been at Jesus' side for three years. They had been very close. He had traveled with Jesus, eaten with Jesus, rowed the boat for Jesus, helped Jesus handle the crowds, and listened to every teaching. Now Peter was in Galilee, and Jesus was not. He was no longer privy to Jesus' plans.

Is it sometimes like that in your life? You can go through seasons when Jesus seems very close. He speaks to you, telling you what to do and where to go. Scripture comes alive. You feel His love all around you. Then suddenly, nothing. Silence. You cannot hear Him, feel Him, or see Him working in your life. You feel deserted by God, and you even begin to wonder if all of this God stuff is real.

You're nodding your head while you read this, aren't you? Maybe you're even feeling an "Amen!" It's hard to stay the course during those times. It becomes crazy easy to quit.

Your thoughts can run wild, and you may begin to waver. It's right for me to tithe, but it's easier to keep the money for myself. It's right for me to pray for those who spread lies about me, but it's easier to curse them out. It's right for me to follow the Word of God, but it's easier to follow the ways of the world. It's right to be a faithful member of my church, but it's easier to walk out the door when things get tough.

Quitting is one of the simplest things you can do in life, even for one of Jesus' closest disciples! Jesus said that He would meet His disciples in Galilee, and He wasn't there. Now they didn't have any idea when or if Jesus would appear. Peter got tired of waiting.

You can tire of waiting for that release, that healing, that promotion, that reconciliation, that peace, that answer. Let me assure you that God makes no mistakes in His timing. Waiting can be frustrating, especially in our current culture of instant gratification. No matter how difficult the waiting is, don't give up. God has more. Don't disqualify yourself. God has not left you or forsaken you (Deuteronomy 31:8; Matthew 28:20).

Jesus said, "Come to me, all you who are weary and burdened, and I will give you rest. Take my yoke upon you and learn from me, for I am gentle and humble in heart, and you will find rest for your souls" (Matthew 11:28–29). If you feel exhausted and burned out, take some time to concentrate on your relationship with Jesus and let Him refresh and restore you.

Wrong Direction

When Peter skipped out, he took others with him. He told them that he was going fishing, and they said, "We'll go with you" (John 21:3).

Your friends and family may also follow you, so be careful. Peter was heading in the wrong direction; you may be, too. Have you left your calling to go fishing? The devil likes nothing better than to get you off the right track. If you've allowed the world's ways to take hold of your mind, your time, and your energy, you aren't following Jesus.

Give back what belongs to Him.

- Let go of the past, "forgetting those things which are behind," as Paul wrote in Philippians 3:13. (NKJV)

- Change your thinking: "Do not conform to the pattern of this world, but be transformed by the renewing of your mind." (Romans 12:2)

- Press into what God has put before you, "reaching forward to those things which are ahead." (Philippians 3:13 NKJV)

A Dilemma

> *They went forth, and entered into a ship immediately; and that night they caught nothing.*
> —*John 21:3 (KJV)*

Let me put this plainly: There's nothing more depressing than catching nothing. Peter and the other disciples learned something important that night. You can't go back to where you were. Now Peter was faced with a dilemma, as you and I often are. Would he keep heading in the wrong direction and taking matters into his own hands instead of waiting on the Lord, even when it brought him a net full of nothing? What was the purpose in that?

The Lord does not want to leave us in a futile struggle, going the wrong way and making no meaningful progress.

> *Early in the morning, Jesus stood on the shore, but the disciples did not realize that it was Jesus.*
>
> *He called out to them, "Friends, haven't you any fish?"*
> —*John 21:4–5*

Do you see the detail hidden in these two verses? The disciples were far enough from Jesus that they couldn't recognize Him, but they were still close enough to hear His voice. This is what it means to "walk by faith, not by sight" (2 Corinthians 5:7 NKJV). Even when you are not sure whether you can see Jesus, you can still trust His voice. You may be heading in the wrong direction because you quit, you got tired of waiting, you went back to what you knew, you were exhausted. But even then, Jesus will call out to you, "Friend, haven't you any fish?"

Jesus told His disciples, "Throw your net on the right side of the boat and you will find some" (John 21:6). The men followed His instruction, and they caught so many fish that they weren't even able to bring in the net.

Peter was a spiritual man. It wasn't lost on him that Jesus had recreated the scene of the day He had first called Peter. The timing was perfect. In a flash, Peter forgot that he had retired. He jumped into the water to swim to shore, leaving the others to bring in the boat. Jesus and His disciples had a small picnic together on the beach. What followed is perhaps one of the most poignant moments in the Bible.

Jesus Reinstates Peter

When they had finished eating, Jesus said to Simon Peter, "Simon son of John, do you love me more than these?"

"Yes, Lord," he said, "you know that I love you."

Jesus said, "Feed my lambs."

Again Jesus said, "Simon son of John, do you love me?"

He answered, "Yes, Lord, you know that I love you."

Jesus said, "Take care of my sheep."

The third time he said to him, "Simon son of John, do you love me?"

> *Peter was hurt because Jesus asked him the third time, "Do you love me?" He said, "Lord, you know all things; you know that I love you."*
>
> *Jesus said, "Feed my sheep. Very truly I tell you, when you were younger you dressed yourself and went where you wanted; but when you are old you will stretch out your hands, and someone else will dress you and lead you where you do not want to go." Jesus said this to indicate the kind of death by which Peter would glorify God. Then he said to him, "Follow me!"*
> **—John 21:15–19**

Peter's three denials were cancelled by three confessions of love. I believe that Jesus looked deep into Peter's eyes as He asked him to follow Him again, even to his death. Peter never again questioned his call. When the Holy Spirit fell on the 120 followers in the upper room, it was Peter who preached the gospel to the Pentecost crowds in Jerusalem (Acts 2:1–41). Three thousand people accepted Jesus and joined the believers that day. Peter, a gifted evangelist, oversaw the church in Jerusalem. He became the rock on which Jesus built His church (Matthew 16:18).

Don't quit in frustration. Wait on the Lord and let Him work in you and on you while you wait. He didn't give up on Peter, and He hasn't given up on you. Remember, His timing is perfect. It is not too late.

> *Therefore, my brothers and sisters, make every effort to confirm your calling and election. For if you do these things, you will never stumble, and you will receive a rich welcome into the eternal kingdom of our Lord and Savior Jesus Christ.*
> **—2 Peter 1:10–11**

Even if you can't see the Lord's face, obey His voice. Read your Bible and pray daily to stir up your hunger for God. Share your thoughts and longings with people you trust. Recall and write down the times in the past when the Lord has led you, and trust that He will continue to lead you. If God has led you before, He will lead you again. Be like Peter and jump out of the boat at the sound of His voice on the shore. Trust, obey, and follow.

WORKBOOK

Chapter Four Questions

Question: Describe a situation in which you were tempted to give up on the Christian life. Has God ever placed you in an extended season of waiting?

_____
_____
_____
_____
_____
_____
_____
_____
_____
_____
_____

Question: When has God seemed far away? What are some things you can do when you are waiting for God's leading and all is silent?

_____
_____
_____
_____
_____
_____
_____
_____
_____
_____

Question: How did Jesus restore and reinstate Peter? Have you ever seen God greatly use a person whom you thought was a lost cause? How has God shown that He won't give up on you?

_____
_____
_____
_____

_____

_____

_____

_____

_____

_____

_____

Action: The Psalms are full of expressions about waiting for God and listening for Him. Pick and memorize a psalm (such as Psalm 25 or 27) that will encourage you during the times when God seems distant.

Chapter Four Notes

CHAPTER FIVE

Developing Our Negatives

Do you remember when digital cameras first became popular? I do. My father and I went to Circuit City (remember Circuit City?), and I told him that I wanted a digital camera.

Now, my father is a tad on the technologically challenged side. He asked the salesperson to let him see one of the cameras. As he was examining it, acting as if he knew what he was doing, he inquired, "Where does the film go?"

My father grew up in the age of 35mm cameras: pop open the back, insert the roll of Kodak film, pull the tab to the other side, and loop it under, taking care not to get any fingerprints on the film. When the salesperson explained that film wasn't necessary for this camera, my father asked, "Well, how do you see the picture? And how do you get it produced?"

The salesperson was kind and patient: "Sir, the minute you take the picture, you can see it on this screen on the back."

In my daddy's generation, you would go to CVS (or to Eckerd's, more likely). You would take the film out of the camera and put it in an envelope with your name on it. At this point, the preliminary images on the film were called "negatives." In other words, when you put the film in the envelope with your name on it, you were taking ownership of your negatives.

Then, in faith, you left your negatives at Eckerd's and trusted that when you came back, they would look different. They would have been through a process to turn them into proper photographs.

What was that process? In order to transform your negatives, they had to be put in a darkroom. A red light was turned on, and the negatives were placed in a tray with a chemical solution over them. While your negatives were being processed, no one else was allowed into the room. The door was locked.

When you are facing a negative situation in your life, and you can't produce something good out of it, God comes along like a photographer. He might confine you to the protection of a darkroom, where no unauthorized persons can enter. You may not be able to see what's happening, and it may seem as though you're not making any progress. But there's a red light burning, like the red blood of Jesus that covers you. And all along, the Lord is applying your solution. You don't know what that solution is made of or what it's called. All you know is that when you emerge from the Lord's solution, your negatives are fixed.

As it so happens, when you hold up your dark, blurry negative to the light, you can see that it is, in fact, the real picture, just not fully developed yet. Oftentimes, we want to keep our negatives face down on the table, but we need to pick them up, hold them up to the light of Christ, and recognize the real picture that's being processed.

Finding yourself in a darkroom doesn't mean that it's the end. There is more for you. You must have faith that the solution in which God is immersing you is the solution you need to be fully produced. You must say, along with Job, "Though he slay me, yet will I hope in him" (Job 13:15).

So, when you would return to Eckerd's a few days later to collect your pictures, they would give you a packet containing a double of every picture, as well as the dark, blurry negatives. Similarly, when the Lord develops you, you're given the full picture—and more—because you trusted the Lord to develop your negatives. You showed faith.

Don't stumble over the negatives in your life. They are not your last stop. They are not the final picture. Remember where you started and how far the Lord has brought you.

My past pushed me into my present. My past made me realize that even though I'm not where I should be, I can still give God praise because He delivered me from what I used to be. Some people won't praise Him until they reach the mountaintop, but we ought to praise Him for bringing us out of the valley!

In Philippians 3:12, Paul encouraged believers to "press on to take hold of that for which Christ Jesus took hold of" them. We ought to remember where we've been, but we can't go back. We must leave our negatives—

doubts, insecurities, failings, naysayers, and haters—behind us and press on toward the life God wants us to experience in His love.

God cannot bless us doubly if we're still holding on to our negatives, the lesser images of ourselves. Like my father dropping off the negatives at Eckerd's, we must trust in God and His process for developing us. He intends more for us if we're patient enough to see it come to fruition.

WORKBOOK

Chapter Five Questions

Question: What are the negatives in your life that need to be processed? In what way might you be experiencing a "darkroom" of God's protection so you can develop fully?

_____
_____
_____
_____
_____
_____
_____
_____
_____
_____
_____

Question: Are you holding tightly to something lesser, a negative? How will you let it go in order to press forward to the greater life and blessing God intends for you?

_____
_____
_____
_____
_____
_____
_____
_____
_____
_____

Action: Write out a prayer for the Lord's wisdom and guidance to help you see your negatives in His light. Ask Him to provide you with insight, but also ask Him to help you trust Him in the process of your development. Ask Him to clarify how you should view your negatives so that you can see His work in your life and praise Him for it.

Chapter Five Notes

CHAPTER SIX

Grace for the Race

Read 2 Corinthians 12:1–10.

Paul was a Pharisee. Paul was brilliant, except he really believed that you could save yourself by following the Law of Moses. You could say that Paul was something of a fanatic.

Jesus' harshest words were directed at Pharisees like Paul. He said that they were "like whitewashed tombs, which look beautiful on the outside but on the inside are full of the bones of the dead and everything unclean" (Matthew 23:27).

It is no wonder that Paul was persecuting those upstart Christians who were preaching heresy against Moses and leading God's chosen people away from Him. In fact, Paul led the charge against followers of Christ. He was fully convinced that he was in the right—until he met the resurrected Jesus on the road to Damascus:

> ...along the road I saw a light from heaven, brighter than the sun, shining around me and those who journeyed with me. And when we all had fallen to the ground, I heard a voice speaking to me and saying in the Hebrew language, "Saul, Saul, why are you persecuting Me? It is hard for you to kick against the goads." So I said, "Who are You, Lord?" And He said, "I am Jesus, whom you are persecuting."
> —*Acts 26:13–15* (NKJV)

That's quite a meeting! Jesus went on to tell Paul that He would send him as His witness to the Gentiles, "to open their eyes, in order to turn them from darkness to light, and from the power of Satan to God" (Acts 26:16–18 NKJV). Paul's surrender was immediate and total. He had been wrong. Now he could make it right.

Except for Jesus Himself, there is no man who casts a bigger shadow in the New Testament than Paul of Tarsus does. Before Paul, Christ's teaching had been reserved for the Jews. It was Paul's life work to change that. His missionary travels throughout Asia Minor fill the book of Acts, and his letters to the Gentile churches are included in the Bible as the best revelation and living out of the Christian faith. Paul even argued on the side of the Gentiles when others wanted to make them submit to circumcision and follow the Law (Galatians 6:12–15).

Being the only apostle in the early Christian church who had not been with Jesus as His disciple, Paul was sometimes challenged to prove that he had the right to call himself an apostle. So, Paul bragged a little about his credentials in a letter to the Corinthian church. Using the third person as a screen for humility, he shared with them some astonishing and indescribable revelations (2 Corinthians 12).

Something to Brag About

Paul would have blown your socks off with the things he could have told you—if he had chosen to do so. In our culture, he could have gone on the writing and speaking circuit and raked in millions, awing and intimidating thousands—if he'd chosen to do so. He could have brought crowds to a speechless state of fascination. He could have acquired quite a following—if he'd chosen to do so.

Paul had seen the resurrected Lord. He had been vaulted into the heavenlies to see unspeakable glories (2 Corinthians 12:2–4). He had been schooled in the Christian faith by the Lord Himself. He was qualified.

He wrote, "Even if I should choose to boast, I would not be a fool, because I would be speaking the truth" (2 Corinthians 12:6). He could have boasted, because he wouldn't have been lying or stretching the truth, but he would rather have talked about his weaknesses (2 Corinthians 12:9).

A Thorn to Humble

> *Therefore, in order to keep me from becoming conceited, I was given a thorn in my flesh, a messenger of Satan, to torment me.*
> **—2 Corinthians 12:7b**

Instead of being given permission to gloat, Paul "was given a thorn" (2 Corinthians 12:7). The Lord told him that this thorn was a gift, and it was sent through Satan. If

I were Paul, I would have had a real problem with this. I would have said indignantly to the Lord, "You mean after all of the things on my ministerial resume, all I've seen, accomplished, written, and preached, Your gift to me is a thorn? You gave me something that will cause me pain? And You sent it through Satan?"

Notice that although Satan brought the thorn to Paul, God was the one who sent it. Herein lies a truth: If God brings you to it, He intends to bring you through it. You may get angry and curse God for your thorns, but your thorns are designed not to break you, but to make you. It's not your titles, accolades, prominence, or prestige that makes you. It's not how well you play or sing or speak or write or teach. What forms and transforms you are the times when you're beaten and the Lord is the one who brings you through.

God never promised that we wouldn't have problems. He promised that He would be with us. The tests, torments, and trials of your life are what will mold you into the likeness of His Son (John 16:33; Romans 8:29).

Paul told us that even Jesus suffered during His life as a man:

> *During the days of Jesus' life on earth, he offered up prayers and petitions with fervent cries and tears to the one who could save him from death, and he was heard because of his reverent submission. Son though he was, he learned obedience from what he suffered....*
> *—Hebrews 5:7–8*

God does not ever intend to hurt us or harm us. His intent is to mold us to be more like Christ. Sometimes that means allowing us to experience things we don't want to experience. Those things move us beyond reliance on our own strengths and abilities and teach us how to depend on God.

Before and After

Do you realize that whenever you look in the mirror, you see a before and an after? Paul did. When he looked in the mirror, he saw a spotless but useless pedigree—his "before"—transformed into an apostolic missionary calling—his "after." He had been a well-recognized leader among the scholars in Jerusalem. But after he met Jesus, he wrote:

> But whatever were gains to me I now consider loss for the sake of Christ. What is more, I consider everything a loss because of the surpassing worth of knowing Christ Jesus my Lord, for whose sake I have lost all things. I consider them garbage, that I may gain Christ and be found in him, not having a righteousness of my own that comes from the law, but that which is through faith in Christ—the righteousness that comes from God on the basis of faith.
> —*Philippians 3:7–9*

When I look in the mirror, I see a person who was broken but is now blessed. I see a person who scraped the bottom of the barrel, only to see later that it was a gift. What do you see? The Holy Spirit must come and rearrange your thoughts, and when He does, it also changes the image you see in the mirror.

Perhaps then you'll see how God strengthened your

walk with Him, how He deepened your prayer life, how He transformed your dealings with people, how He brought you through your crisis, and how you learned to worship Him in the midst of it all. As we recognize that God can use the pain in our lives to transform us, we can find a genuine heart of worship in the midst of suffering.

The Place of Pain

I moved in with my grandmother when I was two months old. She was the first person to teach me the ways of God. She introduced Him to me and taught me how to talk to Him in prayer.

When I was eleven years old, my grandmother began to take ill. She was diagnosed with diabetes, which gradually affected her whole body.

My grandmother passed away the month before my seventeenth birthday. I felt as though my entire world had crumbled, because she had been everything to me. More than just a parental figure, she was my confidant and my friend. I didn't know how I could ever survive losing her.

For a while, I tried to mask and hide from my pain by pursuing the world's riches, but I soon realized that this was in vain. I discovered that running from the pain would never heal me.

Yet, in my weakness, God was strong. His grace preserved me long enough to give me the chance to come back home to Him. My grandmother was still gone, but I realized that the experience had changed me—in key ways, for the better.

My grandmother was my rock. She was the first person

I called when I was in need or trouble. Her transition hurt, but it also cleared the way for me to understand God the way she taught me. I could no longer run to my grandmother and lean on her. I knew the way to God's throne. Now I had no other option but to go to Him personally and build a relationship with Him like I had with my grandmother. I learned that God was able to provide fully where my grandmother was limited. He was able to mend me in ways she could not. He was able to lift me in ways she prayed for but couldn't accomplish herself.

Paul was no stranger to suffering. His thorn was a messenger of Satan sent to buffet him—to torment him, to beat him. No one knows whether this thorn was physical, psychological, or relational. It doesn't matter. The thorn tormented Paul in a place where he already considered himself weak.

This thorn kept Paul totally dependent on God. He could not exalt himself, not one bit, because without the Lord, he was nothing. Paul faced countless trials, beatings, riots, and even stoning. He was accused, belittled, persecuted, and contradicted on the highest order. If Paul had relied on his own power to overcome and succeed, it would have been a hopeless cause.

Demons are real, and each one of them has a specific assignment concerning you. Don't miss the connection here. Sometimes God sends thorns to keep you on course, to keep your feet on the ground and your eyes fixed on Jesus. Sometimes the source of your pain is exactly where the Lord is saying, "If I didn't send this thorn to you, you wouldn't appreciate My power at work in your life."

Has your thorn kept you coming to church, desperate

to hear from the Lord and receive from Him? Has your thorn kept you on your knees in the midnight hour, desperate for the Lord's intervention in your life or in the lives of those you love? Has your thorn kept you digging in the Word of God for direction, encouragement, wisdom, and perspective?

If so, then the place of pain has become a place where you will boast—not in yourself, but in your Lord. But first, you must push through the pain.

Persistent Prayer

> *Three times I pleaded with the Lord to take it away from me. But he said to me, "My grace is sufficient for you, for my power is made perfect in weakness." Therefore I will boast all the more gladly about my weaknesses, so that Christ's power may rest on me.*
> *—2 Corinthians 12:8–9*

Paul didn't just accept the thorn with resignation. He prayed continually and consistently for it to be taken away from him. I don't know about you, but I've been there. I've gone to the Lord in great faith, but when I got up off my knees, my problem was still there. I've asked the Lord to heal somebody I love, but that person still died. I've had a bill due and trusted that the Lord would make a way, but still the lights were turned off and the car was repossessed. I've cried, I've complained, and I've begged.

What option do you have in these situations? When the Lord refused to remove the pain, Paul *praised* Him. The Lord told Paul, "My grace is sufficient for you," and Paul decided to appreciate his weaknesses and hardships for how they provided opportunities for Christ to display His power (2 Corinthians 12:9–10). That might sound crazy to you, but it's what Paul did in the midst of crisis.

David also praised God in times of suffering. In Psalm 13, he said:

> How long, LORD? Will you forget me forever? How long will you hide your face from me? How long must I wrestle with my thoughts and day after day have sorrow in my heart? How long will my enemy triumph over me? ...
>
> But I trust in your unfailing love; my heart rejoices in your salvation. I will sing the LORD's praise, for he has been good to me.
> —*Psalm 13:1–2, 5–6*

Clearly David had been waiting some time for the Lord to deliver him, but he hadn't lost his faith in God's goodness and ultimate deliverance.

You can express your faith by saying to the Lord:

- "I'm still sick, but I'm going to praise You despite my discomfort."
- "This situation grieves me, but I'm going to praise You because You are good."
- "I will glory in my infirmities so that You might get glory out of this situation."

God might not change your situation, but He will change *you* so that you become a stronger believer. You've got to learn how to praise Him anyhow. That's why it's called "a sacrifice of praise" (Hebrews 13:15). You're sacrificing your understanding and your freedom from the situation in order to praise the Lord, no matter what.

> *But those who wait on the LORD shall renew their strength; they shall mount up with wings like eagles, they shall run and not be weary, they shall walk and not faint.*
> *—Isaiah 40:31 (NKJV)*

The Lord's grace is always sufficient. He might not remove you from your situation, but if you will let Him rule and reign in your situation, you will find Him changing you, just as He promised.

WORKBOOK

Chapter Six Questions

Question: What were some of the amazing spiritual blessings given to the apostle Paul? Why did these necessitate the gift of his thorn? What gift has God sent your way that you did not wish to receive?

_____
_____
_____
_____
_____
_____
_____
_____
_____
_____
_____

Question: What was the relationship between God and Satan regarding Paul's thorn? What areas of spiritual warfare are you facing? How can you see God's ultimate control and power over Satan, even amidst these battles?

_____

_____

_____

_____

_____

_____

_____

_____

_____

Question: What was God's response to Paul's persistent prayer for his thorn to be removed? How have you experienced God's sufficient grace when the answer to your earnest prayers was "no"?

_____

_____

_____

_____
_____
_____
_____
_____
_____
_____
_____
_____

Action: Think of someone you know who is facing a spiritual battle or a painful thorn in his or her life right now. Plan a way to encourage this person. What is a tangible act of kindness you can do for this person as an expression of God's sufficient and abundant grace to help him or her during this time of difficulty?

Chapter Six Notes

CONCLUSION

The Lord Is on Your Side

> *"If it had not been the LORD who was on our side," let Israel now say—"If it had not been the LORD who was on our side, when men rose up against us, then they would have swallowed us alive, when their wrath was kindled against us; then the waters would have overwhelmed us, the stream would have gone over our soul; then the swollen waters would have gone over our soul."*
>
> *Blessed be the LORD, who has not given us as prey to their teeth. Our soul has escaped as a bird from the snare of the fowlers; the snare is broken, and we have escaped. Our help is in the name of the LORD, who made heaven and earth.*
> —***Psalm 124*** *(NKJV)*

You are lost without the Lord on your side. You can take this truth to the eternal bank. The Lord has more in store for you than you can "ask or imagine" (Ephesians 3:20), but you must not forget that all of the provision is from Him and that you continually need His sufficient grace.

Even your desire to follow Jesus is a gift from the Lord. You are compelled, drawn, and lured by Him into His presence and the life He desires for you (John 6:44). If the Lord God had not been on your side, you would not even want to follow Him and receive more for your life.

The Lord's plan for you is perfect, even when it looks absurd. No human reasoning would ever have approved of Gideon's small and oddly equipped army against the numerous, well-equipped Midianites (Judges 7:16–18). But the Lord was on their side! Gideon's small band of committed, loud, trumpet-toting soldiers "escaped as a bird from the snare of the fowlers" (Psalm 124:7 NKJV). With the Lord on your side, long odds of success turn into greater praise after the victory.

Maybe you're not facing external enemies, but rather an army of negative and subservient thoughts in your mind. Put your trust in the General leading your battle, who has never lost a fight. There will be times when you come to a crossroads of fact and faith. Faith is the route that will always lead you to a successful victory. The more you trust now, the more you will triumph later.

As you seek God, you will encounter giants. As my old preacher used to say, "If you don't meet the devil head-on, you're probably going his way!" Giants don't discriminate, and they don't play fair. But with the Lord on your side, you will slay the giant in the power, the way, and the name of the Almighty, just as that ruddy-faced shepherd boy (and lunch delivery person) David did. "Blessed be the LORD, who has not given us as prey to their teeth" (Psalm 124:6 NKJV).

You may be facing a giant right now in your life and feeling overwhelmed and discouraged. You may feel that you won't overcome this one. I dare you to trust what is in your hand. Trust what you have been given. It does not matter if it seems small or inferior. You have exactly what it takes to overcome your giant. Remember, there's greater in you than what you're facing.

Like the invalid at Bethesda, sometimes you don't even know how to respond to the Lord Jesus' simple offer for healing. Only the Holy Spirit quickens and awakens within you a longing for the Lord's touch (1 Corinthians 2:14).

The Lord comes alongside you even when you stray. Even when you retire from His calling and turn back to your old life like Peter turned back to fishing, He does not give up on you. The Lord was on Peter's side, calling out to him, "Throw your net on the right side…" (John 21:6). The Lord remains within earshot, even when we don't feel His presence. The Lord is with us, and "we have escaped" (Psalm 124:7 NKJV) from our backsliding ways.

God's strength is with you when you are weak. Even in those deeply dark moments of despair, God is with you. Even in those silent, still, fear-filled nights, God is with you. Just when it seems as though you have exhausted all hope and measures, God is with you. Not only is He with you, but He is willing, able, and ready to accept you back into His fold, where you belong.

The Lord is right there with you, delivering all-sufficient grace, when you are recoiling from the thorn He sent. He keeps you humble, dependent upon and seeking Him, remembering that "our help is in the name of the LORD, who made heaven and earth" (Psalm 124:8). Even when the answer to your fervent prayers is "no," your faith grows as you learn to offer your sacrifice of praise in the midst of your pain.

If it were not for Him, where and what would you be?

When you want the life God intends for you all of your days—when you build armies, when you face giants, when you turn your back, when you wince at thorns—the Lord, who made heaven and earth, is on your side as you walk in His ways.

> *No, in all these things we are more than conquerors through him who loved us. For I am convinced that neither death nor life, neither angels nor demons, neither the present nor the future, nor any powers, neither height nor depth, nor anything else in all creation, will be able to separate us from the love of God that is in Christ Jesus our Lord.*
> *—Romans 8:37–39*

As you look at your life and the world around you and you think, "There has to be more," know this: There is more. It is in the mighty hand of your good heavenly Father. Follow Him wholeheartedly, obey His commandments, and walk into the fullness of life Christ came to bring you (John 10:10).

REFERENCES

Notes

1. Strong, James. "G5217 – hypagō." *Strong's Exhaustive Concordance of the Bible*. Hunt & Eaton, 1894. In *Blue Letter Bible*. https://www.blueletterbible.org/lang/lexicon/lexicon.cfm?t=kjv&strongs=g5217.

About the Author

Darius L. Francis works adamantly to help individuals get to where they desire to be. His journey started in Miami, Florida, when he became an avid, ambitious minister and evangelist at the age of 16. It was in middle Tennessee where his ministry took flight and he endured much spiritual growth. He teaches that success is not birthed overnight; it is a process that has no shortcuts.

D. L. Francis served as the senior pastor of the Grace Empowerment Fellowship Baptist Church and then of

New Genesis of Atlanta until he was led to move beyond the walls of the sanctuary. Now, as a national Christian life coach, teacher, trainer, and speaker, he teaches workshops and seminars and serves as a keynote speaker and coach. He aids in personal and professional growth through the study and practical application of proven methods.

His passion extends beyond his decade of experience in public speaking. In traveling around the world to speak, coach, and train, he has motivated countless individuals to pursue their passions and walk in their purpose. He is on a mission to help people awaken their inner drive and dive into their destiny. As an entrepreneur and renaissance man, he has a Certificate in Entrepreneurship Essentials from Harvard Business School Online.

According to D.L. Francis, "If the sky is your limit, then you're aiming too low."

About Sermon To Book

SermonToBook.com began with a simple belief: that sermons should be touching lives, *not* collecting dust. That's why we turn sermons into high-quality books that are accessible to people all over the globe.

Turning your sermon series into a book exposes more people to God's Word, better equips you for counseling, accelerates future sermon prep, adds credibility to your ministry, and even helps make ends meet during tight times.

John 21:25 tells us that the world itself couldn't contain the books that would be written about the work of Jesus Christ. Our mission is to try anyway. Because in heaven, there will no longer be a need for sermons or books. Our time is now.

If God so leads you, we'd love to work with you on your sermon or sermon series.

Visit www.sermontobook.com to learn more.

www.ingramcontent.com/pod-product-compliance
Lightning Source LLC
LaVergne TN
LVHW020937090426
835512LV00020B/3398